MATH FOR MINECRAFTERS

Adventures in Multiplication & Division

Illustrated by Amanda Brack

Sky Pony Press
New York

Sky Pony Press books may be purchased in bulk at special discounts for sales promotion, corporate gifts, fund-raising, or educational purposes. Special editions can also be created to specifications. For details, contact the Special Sales Department, Sky Pony Press, 307 West 36th Street, 11th Floor, New York, NY 10018 or info@skyhorsepublishing.com.

Sky Pony® is a registered trademark of Skyhorse Publishing, Inc.®, a Delaware corporation.

Minecraft® is a registered trademark of Notch Development AB.
The Minecraft game is copyright © Mojang AB.

Visit our website at www.skyponypress.com.

Authors, books, and more at SkyPonyPressBlog.com.

10 9 8 7 6 5 4 3 2

Cover design by Brian Peterson

Cover and interior art by Amanda Brack

Book design by Kevin Baier

Print ISBN: 978-1-5107-1820-3

Printed in China

A NOTE TO PARENTS

When you want to reinforce classroom skills at home, it's crucial to have kid-friendly learning materials. This *Math for Minecrafters* workbook transforms math practice into an irresistible adventure complete with diamond swords, zombies, skeletons, and creepers. That means less arguing over homework and more fun overall.

Math for Minecrafters is also fully aligned with National Common Core Standards for 3rd and 4th grade math. What does that mean, exactly? All of the problems in this book correspond to what your child is expected to learn in school. This eliminates confusion and builds confidence for greater homework-time success!

As an added benefit to parents, the pages of this workbook are color-coded to help you target specific skill areas as needed. Each color represents one of the four categories of Common Core math instruction. Use the chart below to guide you in understanding the different skills being taught at your child's school and to pinpoint areas where he or she may need extra practice.

BLUE	Operations and Algebraic Thinking
PINK	**Numbers and Operations in Base 10**
GREEN	Measurement and Data
ORANGE	Geometry

As the workbook progresses, the math problems become more advanced. Encourage your child to progress at his or her own pace. Learning is best when students are challenged, but not frustrated. What's most important is that your Minecrafter is engaged in his or her own learning.

Whether it's the joy of seeing their favorite game characters on every page or the thrill of solving challenging problems just like Steve and Alex, there is something in this workbook to entice even the most reluctant math student.

Happy adventuring!

MULTIPLICATION BY GROUPING

Write the multiplication sentence that matches the picture.
Then solve the equation.

Example:

1.

Answer:

$$2 \times 10 = 20$$

2. ____ x ____ = ____

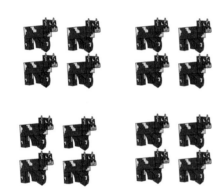

3. ____ x ____ = ____

4. ____ x ____ = ____

5. ____ x ____ = ____

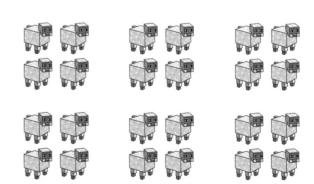

MYSTERY MESSAGE
WITH MULTIPLICATION

Multiply. Then use the letters to fill in the blanks below and reveal the answer to the joke.

1. 4 x 8 = 32   A   **6.** 8 x 5 = ___   O

2. 2 x 6 = ___   D   **7.** 8 x 2 = ___   E

3. 6 x 3 = ___   Y   **8.** 9 x 6 = ___   R

4. 3 x 8 = ___   C   **9.** 10 x 3 = ___   T

5. 7 x 5 = ___   S

Q: Where does a baby creeper go when his parents are at work?
COPY THE LETTERS FROM THE ANSWERS ABOVE TO FIND OUT.

He goes ___ ___
         30   40

         A   A
       ___ ___ ___ ___ ___ ___ ___ ___
       12 32 18 35 24 32 54 16

ZOMBIE'S GUIDE TO PLACE VALUE

Write the number on each zombie in expanded form in the space provided.

Example:

1.  1,360

Answer:

1,000 + 300 + 60 + 0

2.  4,672

_____

3.  2,798

_____

4.  8,540

_____

5.  3,151

_____

6.  6,736

_____

7.  5,459

_____

MATH FACTS CHALLENGE

Find the pattern and fill in the empty spaces to help Alex escape the zombie.

7

14

28

56

84

TELLING TIME

Look at the clocks below and write the time in the space provided:

Example:

1.

Answer: 2:15

2.

Answer: _____

3.

Answer: _____

4.

Answer: _____

5.

Answer: _____

6.

Answer: _____

THE TRADING TABLE

The villagers have emeralds to give Alex in exchange for her food items. Look at the table below to solve the problems that follow.

FARMER	🟢	🟢	🟢	🟢			
LIBRARIAN	🟢	🟢					
BLACKSMITH	🟢	🟢	🟢				
BUTCHER	🟢	🟢	🟢	🟢	🟢	🟢	

Write the amount of emeralds next to each villager using the table above.

1 pile of emeralds = 8 emeralds.

1. The **farmer** villager has _____ .

2. The **librarian** villager has _____ .

3. The **blacksmith** villager has _____ .

4. The **butcher** villager has _____ .

5. Which villagers have more emeralds than the **blacksmith** villager? _____

6. Which villager has the least amount of emeralds? _____

7. The **librarian** wants to have as many emeralds as the **butcher**. Which villager's collection does he need to add to his? _____

GEOMETRY SKILLS PRACTICE

How many items are in each array? Count the number of items in one row and one column. Write a multiplication sentence to find the answer.

Example:

1. $\underline{2} \times \underline{5} = \underline{10}$

2. _____ × _____ = _____

3. _____ × _____ = _____

4. _____ × _____ = _____

5. _____ × _____ = _____

6. ___ x ___ = ___

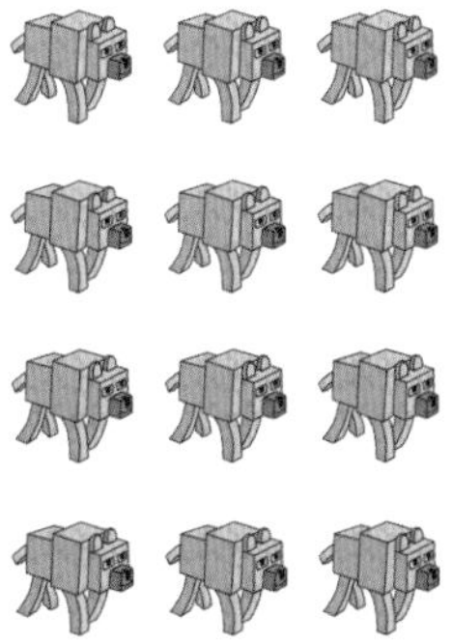

7. ___ x ___ = ___

8. ___ x ___ = ___

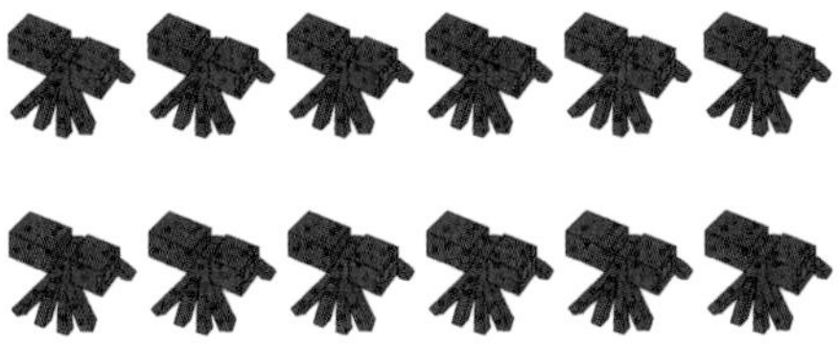

9. ___ x ___ = ___

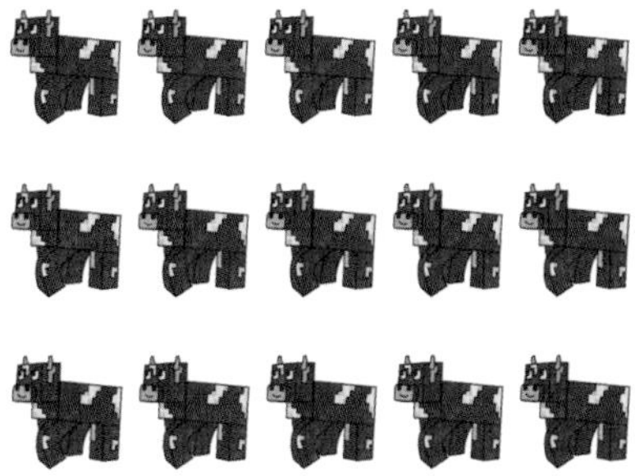

HARDCORE MODE: Try this hardcore math challenge!

___ x ___ = ___ + ___ = ___

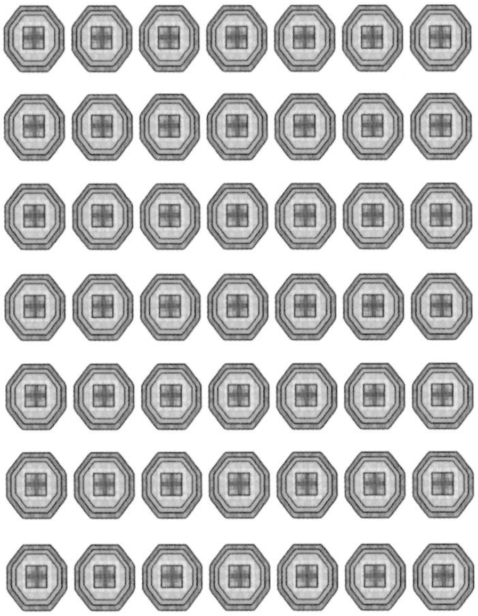

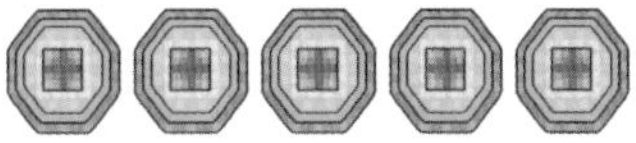

MULTIPLICATION WORD PROBLEMS

Read the problem carefully. Draw a picture or write a number sentence to help you solve the problem.

Example:

1. A creeper blows up 2 cows every time it explodes. How many cows will be killed by 3 exploding creepers?

Answer: 6 COWS

$$3 \times 2 = 6$$

2. In order to make 1 cake, you need 3 buckets of milk. How many buckets of milk do you need to make 2 cakes?

Answer: _____

3. One block of wood is enough to make 4 planks of wood. If you have 4 blocks of wood, how many planks can you make?

Answer: _____

4. One ocelot drops 3 experience orbs for you to collect. How many experience orbs can you collect from 6 ocelots?

Answer: _____

5. You need 6 sandstone blocks to craft 1 set of stairs. How many sandstone blocks do you need to build 7 sets of stairs?

Answer: _____

6. One cow drops 3 pieces of raw beef. How many pieces of raw beef can you get from 4 cows?

Answer: _____

7. One full day in the game world is the same as 20 minutes in the real world. If you spend 5 days in Alex's world, how many real-world minutes go by?

Answer: _____

8. Steve needs 9 fish to tame an ocelot. How many fish does he need to tame 3 ocelots?

Answer: _____

9. It takes 4 bottles of potion to survive a hostile mob attack. How many bottles of potion do you need to survive 6 mob attacks?

Answer: _____

GHAST'S GUIDE TO PLACE VALUE

Answer the multiplication questions below.
Then round to the closest ten.

	Solve It!	**Round It!**
1. 2 x 3 =	6	10

2. 4 x 9 = _____ _____

3. 6 x 8 = _____ _____

4. 3 x 5 = _____ _____

5. 7 x 4 = _____ _____

6. 8 x 5 = _____ _____

7. 9 x 7 = _____ _____

MATH FACTS CHALLENGE

Count by 4 and practice your math facts to help Steve escape the wither!

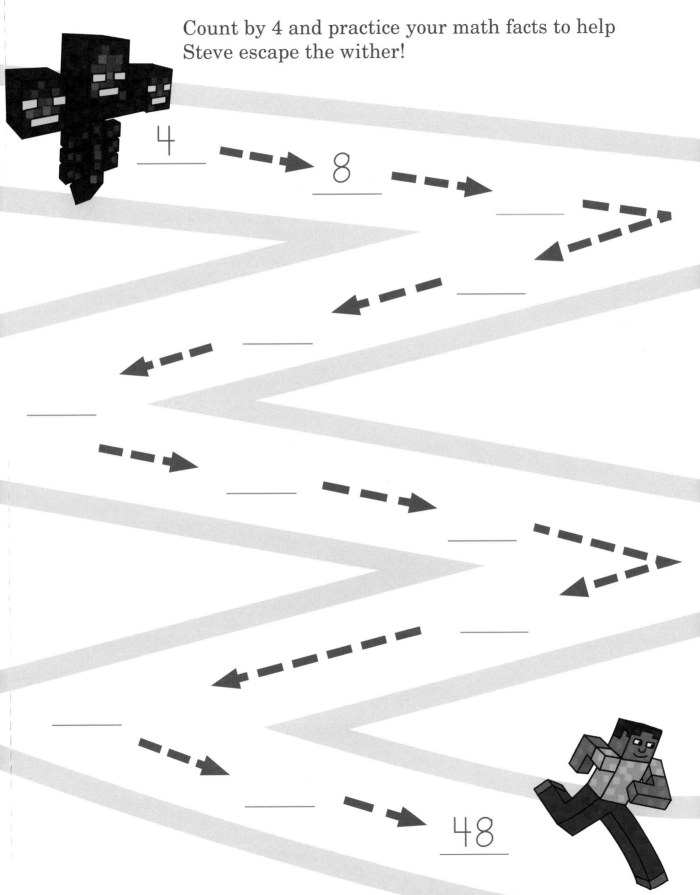

4

8

48

MINUTE HAND MYSTERY

A computer glitch erased the minute hands from these clocks! Solve the problem to find out how many minutes have passed, then draw in the minute hand.

Solve it.

Draw it.

1. 10 ÷ 2 = ___5___ minutes

2. 15 x 3 = _____ minutes

3. 60 ÷ 4 = _____ minutes

4. 20 x 2 = _____ minutes

5. 11 x 5 = _____ minutes

6. 75 ÷ 3 = _____ minutes

EQUAL TRADE

This librarian villager loves trading for new coins. Figure out the right number of coins to trade so that you don't lose any money in the deal.

1. How many **pennies** equal 1 dime?   Answer: _____

2. How many **nickels** equal 1 quarter?      Answer: _____

3. How many **pennies** equal 3 nickels?      Answer: _____

4. How many **quarters** equal a dollar?   Answer: _____

5. How many **dimes** equal 2 quarters?   Answer: _____

ADVENTURES IN GEOMETRY

Which of these gaming images are symmetrical? Circle them.

Symmetrical = an object that can be divided with a line into two matching halves.

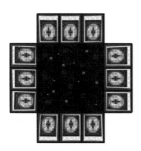

CREATIVE MODE

Complete the other half of this drawing to make it as symmetrical as possible:

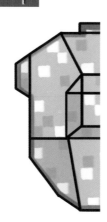

SHELTER GEOMETRY

Alex and Steve have been working all afternoon to build a new shelter out of redstone blocks.

Area=
height x width

1. Calculate the area of Alex's wall:

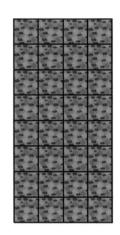

_____ x _____ = _____

2. Calculate the area of Steve's wall:

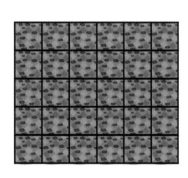

_____ x _____ = _____

3. Which player's wall has the greatest area? _____

4. How many more blocks did that player use? _____

5. If you combine their two walls, what would the area of their new, larger wall be? _____

19

MULTIPLICATION BY GROUPING

Count each group of 3, then finish the equation to find the answer.

1. _____ x 3 = _____

2. _____ x 3 = _____

3. _____ x 3 = _____

4. _____ x 3 = _____

5. _____ x 3 = _____

MYSTERY MESSAGE
WITH MULTIPLICATION AND DIVISION

Solve the problems below to find out which number matches with which letter. Then put the correct letters into the message to answer the riddle!

1. $234 \div 2 =$ 117   E

2. $34 \times 3 =$ O

3. $77 \times 4 =$ H

4. $434 \div 7 =$ R

5. $165 \times 5 =$ B

6. $924 \div 4 =$ N

7. $201 \times 3 =$ I

Q: What mysterious character looks like Steve but has glowing white eyes?

COPY THE LETTERS FROM THE ANSWERS ABOVE TO FIND OUT.

308   117   62   102   825   62   603   231   117

ENDERMAN'S GUIDE TO PLACE VALUE

Solve the multiplication equations below. Match each answer to the correct place value description on the right.

1. 12 x 4 = 36 **A.** 2 hundreds

2. 8 x 8 = _____   **B.** 6 ones

3. 9 x 9 = _____   **C.** 7 tens

4. 10 x 20 = _____   **D.** 3 tens

5. 8 x 9 = _____   **E.** 4 ones

6. 11 x 5 = _____   **F.** 8 tens

7. 5 x 6 = _____   **G.** 5 ones

SKIP COUNT CHALLENGE

Thanks to the lure enchantment, you catch 9 pufferfish every time you go fishing! Pretty soon, you'll have enough to tame your ocelot. Count by 9 to find out how many pufferfish you'll catch at the end of the day.

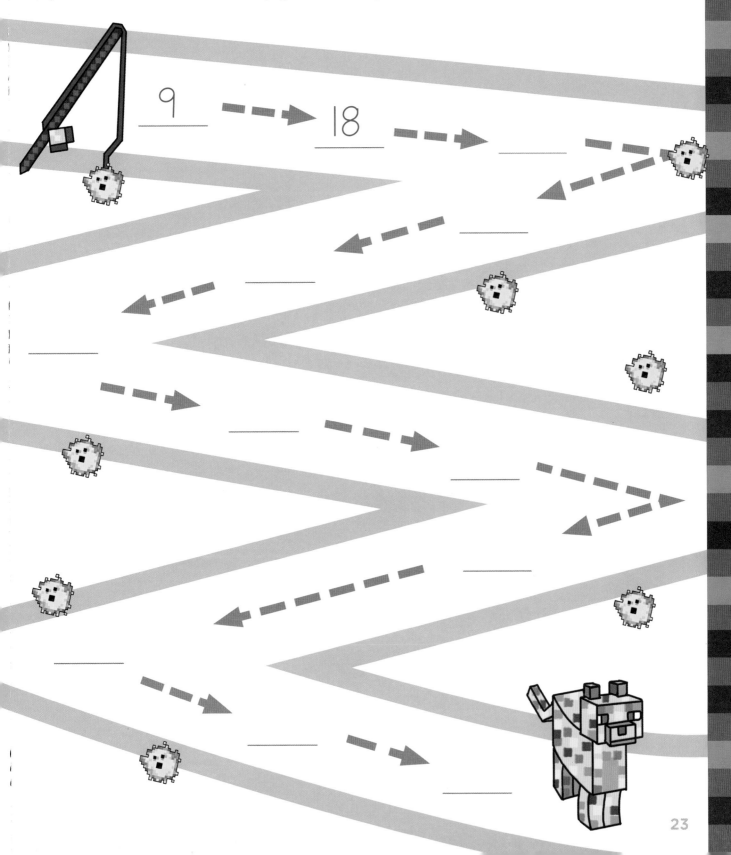

TELLING TIME

The mooshroom is teaching his baby how to tell time, but he needs your help. Help the baby mooshroom by writing down the correct time next to each clock.

Example:

1.

Answer: 3:25

2.

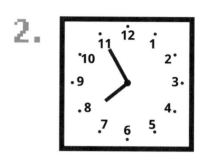

Answer: _____

3.

Answer: _____

4.

Answer: _____

5.

Answer: _____

6.

Answer: _____

7.

Answer: _____

8.

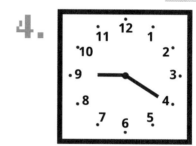

Answer: _____

SPAWN EGG CHALLENGE

Solve the equations next to each colored bucket to find out how many exploding creepers will soon be hatching from the buckets. Then run!

 1. 27 x 5 = _____

 2. 120 ÷ 6 = _____

 3. 94 x 2 = _____

 4. 39 x 2 = _____

 5. 320 ÷ 8 = _____

 6. 53 x 4 = _____

7. Which colored bucket has the most creeper eggs? _____

8. Which two colored buckets, when combined, add up to 228 creeper eggs? _____ and _____

HARDCORE MODE: Try this hardcore math challenge!

9. What is the sum of all the creeper eggs? _____

EQUAL PARTS CHALLENGE

Use a ruler or the edge of a piece of paper to help you draw partitions in the shapes below.

When you partition something, you divide it into sections

1. The first gold ingot below is partitioned, or divided, into two equal parts with the red line.

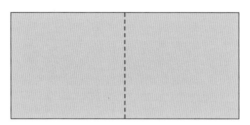

There is another way to divide this gold ingot into two equal, symmetrical parts.
Draw it below:

Use your pencil to shade in one of the pieces above.
What fraction describes this picture? _____

2. Partition the iron ingot into **3** equal shares in two different ways.

Use your pencil to shade in one of the pieces above. What fraction describes this picture? _____

3. Partition the iron ingot into **4** equal shares in two different ways.

Use your pencil to shade in one of the pieces above. What fraction describes this picture? _____

MYSTERY MESSAGE WITH MULTIPLICATION

Solve each multiplication equation below. Use the answers to solve the riddle.

1. 57
   ×9
   ___
   513

   A

2. 72
   ×5
   ___

   G

3. 27
   ×9
   ___

   Q

4. 57
   ×6
   ___

   S

5. 41
   ×6
   ___

   N

6. 46
   ×8
   ___

   U

7. 84
   ×4
   ___

   E

8. 26
   ×9
   ___

   C

9. 50
   ×7
   ___

   D

10. 78
    ×6
    ___

    I

11. 41
    ×8
    ___

    R

Q: What is Steve's favorite type of dancing?
COPY THE LETTERS FROM THE ANSWERS ABOVE TO FIND OUT.

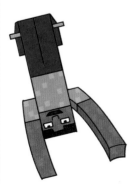

342 243 368 513 328 336

350 513 246 234 468 246 360

MULTIPLICATION AND DIVISION MYSTERY NUMBER

Some hacker has replaced a number from each of the below equations with a TNT block. Use multiplication and division to solve for the missing numbers.

1. 3 × = 24   = 8

2. ÷ 8 = 6   =

3. 120 ÷ = 12   =

4. 3 × = 21   =

5. 45 ÷ = 9   =

6. × 9 = 36   =

7. 12 ÷ = 3   =

8. × 12 = 60   =

9. 27 ÷ = 9   =

10. 42 ÷ = 6   =

SNOW GOLEM'S NUMBER CHALLENGE

Match the Snow Golem with the description of the number.

1. Hundreds: **1** Tens: **2** Ones: **9**

642÷2

2. Hundreds: **3** Tens: **2** Ones: **1**

51x8

3. Hundreds: **1** Tens: **7** Ones: **5**

26x9

4. Hundreds: **4** Tens: **0** Ones: **8**

875÷5

5. Hundreds: **2** Tens: **3** Ones: **4**

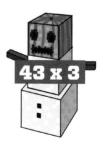
43 x 3

SKIP COUNT CHALLENGE

A rare but hostile chicken jockey is headed your way!
Solve the equation and count by the answer to escape.

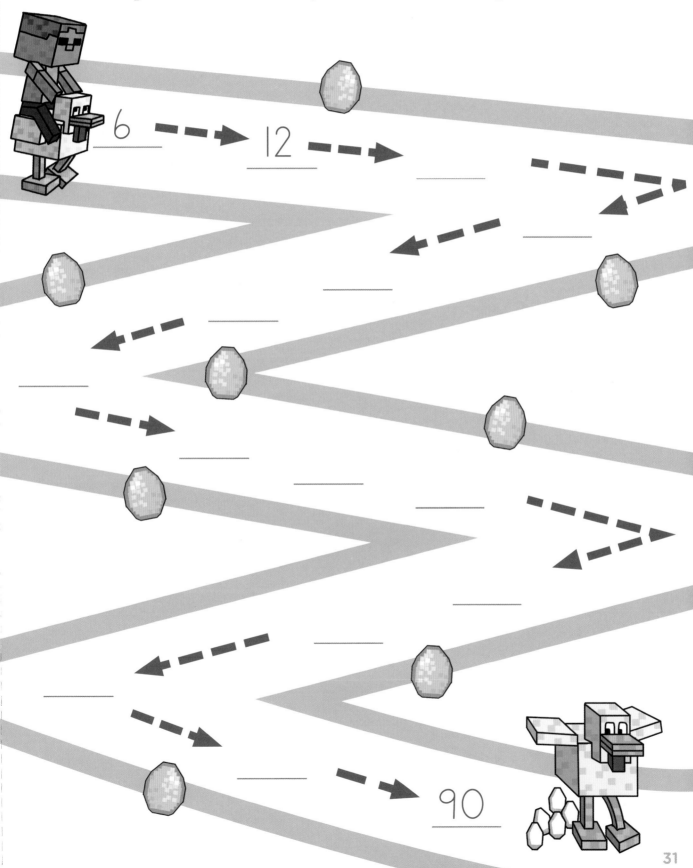

_6_ ➡ 12 ➡ ____

____ ____

____ ____

____ ____

____ ____

____ 90

CREATING POTIONS

Use the recipes below to figure out the number of items needed to make more of each potion.

1. ![bottle] = 3 awkward potions + 3 glistering melons

![three bottles] = _____ awkward potions +

_____ glistering melons

2. ![bottle] = 2 awkward potions + 5 sugars

![four bottles] = _____ awkward potions + _____ sugars

3. ![bottle] = 7 golden carrots + 9 nether warts

![six bottles] = _____ golden carrots +

_____ nether warts

INVISIBILITY POTION FORMULA

4. 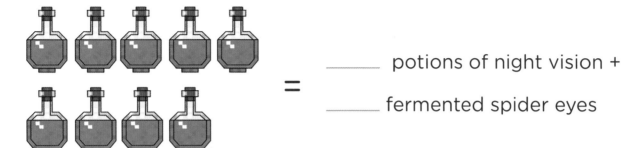 = 4 potions of night vision + 7 fermented spider eyes

_____ potions of night vision +

_____ fermented spider eyes

INVISIBILITY POTION INGREDIENTS TABLE

Use the formula above to determine how much you need of each ingredient below. The first one is done for you.

Night Vision Potion	8			
Fermented Spider Eyes				

ADVENTURES IN GEOMETRY: PERIMETER AND AREA

Steve is building new rooms in his house. Multiply the number of blocks to help him find the perimeter and area of the walls.

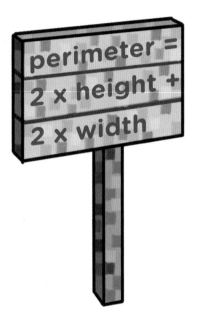

perimeter =
2 x height +
2 x width

1. Perimeter = _____

If Steve doubles the height of this wall,

what would the new perimeter be? _____

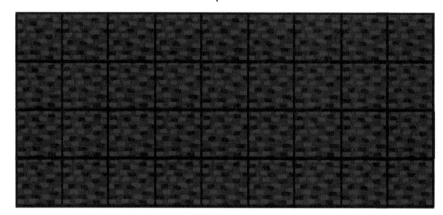

2. Perimeter = _____

If Steve destroys the right half of this wall, what would the new perimeter be? _____

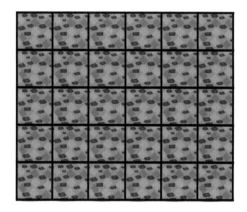

3. Perimeter = _____

Alex built a wall twice as wide as this one. What was the perimeter of her new wall?

_____

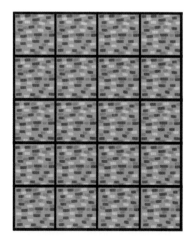

area = height × width

4. Area = _____

If Steve doubles the height of this wall, what would the new area be? _____

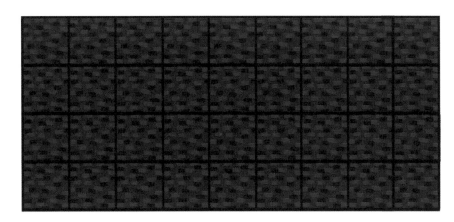

5. Area = _____

If Steve destroys the right half of this wall, what would the new area be? _____

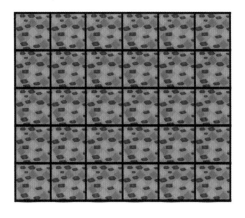

6. Area = _____

Alex built a wall twice as big as this one. What was the area of her wall? _____

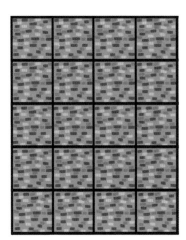

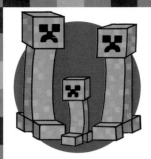

WORD PROBLEMS

Use multiplication and division to solve these word problems.

1. Alex is planning to get carrots for her horses. She has 32 horses and each horse needs 8 carrots a day. How many carrots does she need to feed the horses each day?

Answer: _____

2. Steve plants melon seeds in his garden. He figures out that 3 seeds make one melon. If his garden made 48 melons, how many seeds did he plant?

Answer: _____

3. You destroy 12 Endermen with your iron sword! If each Enderman drops 4 Ender pearls when he dies, how many pearls do you collect?

Answer: _____

4. Baby zombies are spawning! You spot 16 little green zombies total. If you encounter 3 more groups of 16 baby zombies, how many zombies will you encounter in all?

Answer: _____

5. Steve needs to feed his mooshrooms and baby mooshrooms. Each adult needs 2 wheat items, while each baby needs just 1 wheat item. If he has 12 adult mooshrooms and 5 baby mooshrooms, how many wheat items does he need to feed them?

Answer: _____

6. Escape the charged creepers! If it takes you 6 minutes to row your wooden boat 9 feet, how long do you estimate it will take you to row across a river that is 54 feet wide?

Answer: _____

7. Steve has 68 blocks of redstone that he needs to transport to his house. If 2 blocks can fit in his mining cart during each trip, how many trips will he have to take to move them all?

Answer: _____

8. You want to make cookies for all of your favorite players. You need 2 wheat items to make each batch of cookies. If you make 63 batches of cookies, how many wheat items do you need?

Answer: _____

PLACE VALUE

Match the answer to each equation on the left with the number of emeralds on the right to help Steve calculate how many emeralds total he mined on a certain day.

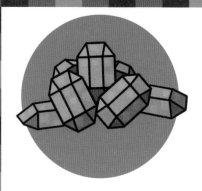

1. 3 x 12 x 5 = ___

A.
405

2. 9 x 22 x 4 = ___

B.
630

3. 15 x 3 x 9 = ___

C.
576

4. 7 x 14 x 6 = ___

D.
180

5. 6 x 24 x 4 = ___

E.
588

6. 2 x 35 x 9 = ___

F.
208

7. 13 x 8 x 2 = ___

G.
792

GHASTLY NUMBER CHALLENGE

Match the answer to the Ghast's equation on the right with the correct place value description on the left.

1. Hundreds: **9** Tens: **1** Ones: **2**

44 x 7

2. Hundreds: **6** Tens: **7** Ones: **2**

76 x 10

3. Hundreds: **3** Tens: **0** Ones: **8**

24 x 38

4. Hundreds: **2** Tens: **2** Ones: **0**

2200 ÷ 10

5. Hundreds: **7** Tens: **6** Ones: **0**

498 ÷ 2

6. Hundreds: **2** Tens: **4** Ones: **9**

42 x 16

7. Hundreds: **5** Tens: **2** Ones: **0**

26 x 20

MOB MEASUREMENTS

Find out how many inches tall each mob is using multiplication and addition.

1 foot = 12 inches

Example:

1.

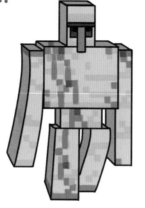

Iron Golem

3 feet, 4 inches

12 x 3 = <u>36</u> inches

36 + 4 = <u>40</u> inches tall

2.

Zombie

2 feet, 6 inches

Height in inches = _____

3.

Skeleton

3 feet, 1 inch

Height in inches = _____

4.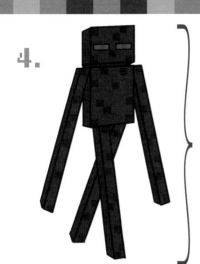

Enderman

4 feet, 3 inches

Height in inches = _____

5.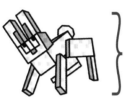

Rabbit

1 foot, 6 inches

Height in inches = _____

METRIC MEASUREMENTS

Complete the chart using the formula provided.

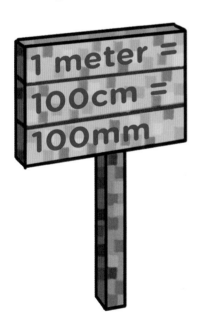

1 meter =
100cm =
100mm

	Length in meters	Length in cm	Length in mm
	2	200	2,000
		400	
	1.5		1,500
			2,500
	1		

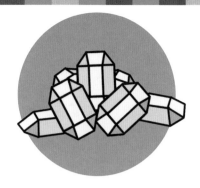

ADVENTURES IN GEOMETRY

Identify the angle shown in each picture as acute, right, or obtuse.

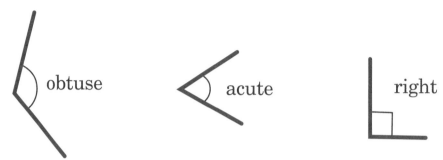

obtuse   acute   right

1. _____   2. _____

3. _____   4. _____

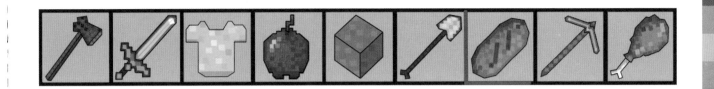

5. _____

6. _____   **7.** _____

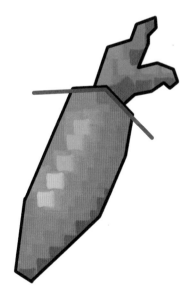

8. _____   **9.** _____

MULTIPLICATION AND DIVISION MYSTERY NUMBER

A troublesome creeper has replaced a number in each equation with a creeper spawn egg! Use multiplication and division to determine the missing number.

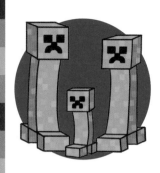

1. $217 \div$  $= 31$  $=$ _____

2.  $\div 5 = 85$  $=$ _____

3. $548 \div 4 =$     $=$ _____

4. $424 \div$  $= 4$  $=$ _____

5. $48 \div 6 =$     $=$ _____

6.  $\div 3 = 126$  $=$ _____

7. $72 \div$  $= 9$  $=$ _____

8. $512 \div 8 =$     $=$ _____

9. $9 \times$  $= 702$  $=$ _____

MYSTERY MESSAGE
WITH MULTIPLICATION AND DIVISION

Solve the multiplication and division problems below. Then write the letters in the blank spaces at the bottom of the page to get the answer to the joke!

1. $892 \div 2 =$ _____   G

2. $45 \times 8 =$ _____   B

3. $623 \div 7 =$ _____   I

4. $1122 \div 6 =$ _____   N

5. $91 \times 9 =$ _____   O

6. $230 \times 4 =$ _____   X

Q: What is a Minecrafter's favorite sport?

COPY THE LETTERS FROM THE ANSWERS ABOVE TO FIND OUT.

Answer:

360   819   920   89   187   446

SKELETON'S GUIDE TO PLACE VALUE

Solve the division equations below to fill in the empty place value box beside each one.

1. 917 ÷ 7 = _____

Hundreds

2. 255 ÷ 5 = _____

Ones

3. 1,473 ÷ 3 = _____

Tens

4. 336 ÷ 24 = _____

Ones

5. 425 ÷ 5 = _____

Tens

6. 2,004 ÷ 4 = _____

Hundreds

7. 1,602 ÷ 6 = _____

Ones

SKIP COUNT CHALLENGE

A mob of zombie villagers has discovered you in the forest! Figure out the number pattern and fill in the blanks to complete the path before the villagers can catch you.

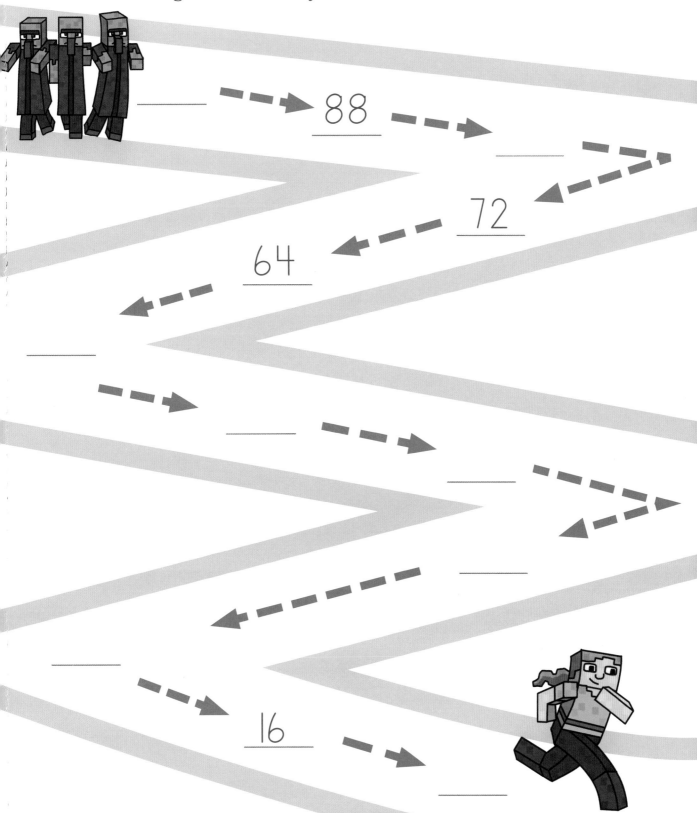

_____ → 88 → _____

72 ← _____

64 ←

_____

_____ →

_____ →

_____ →

_____ ←

_____

16 →

_____

ANIMAL TALLY

Use the six clues below to help you fill in the chart on the right-hand page.

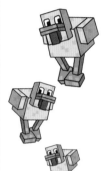

1. If Steve can fit 6 chickens at each of his farms and he has 2 farms full of chickens, plus 2 extra chickens that he keeps in his house, how many chickens total does he have?

2. If Alex has 4 times as many chickens as Steve, how many does she have?

3. If Steve has 51 horses and Alex has $\frac{1}{3}$ the amount that he has, how many horses does she have?

4. If Steve has 13 sheep and Alex has 4 times that number of sheep, how many sheep does she have?

5. If Steve has 5 groups of 20 cows and horses combined, how many cows does he have?

6. If Alex has $\frac{1}{7}$ the amount of cows as Steve, how many cows does she have total?

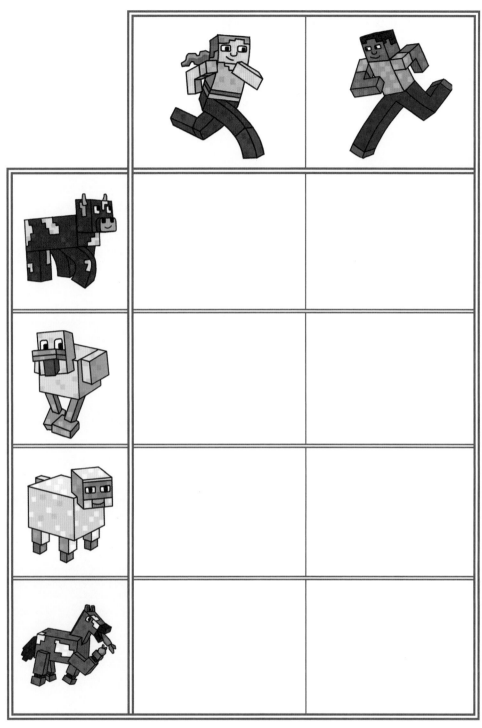

ADVENTURES IN GEOMETRY

Label the red lines on each image as parallel, perpendicular, or intersecting.

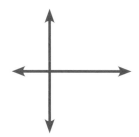

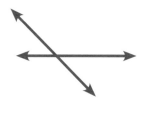

Parallel Lines   **Perpendicular Lines**   **Intersecting Lines**

1. _____

2. _____

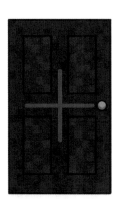

3. _____

4. _____

5. _____

6. _____

7. _____

WORD PROBLEMS

Use multiplication, division, addition, and subtraction to solve these word problems.

1. Each pickaxe in your inventory bar digs up 5 diamonds before breaking. You dig up 4,650 diamonds total. How many pickaxes did you use?

2. You are hiding from 42 hostile mobs. Half of them are 8-legged cave spiders. The other half are 2-legged skeletons. How many legs are there in this angry group of mobs?

3. Steve has a collection of mining carts. Each cart can hold 7 redstone blocks inside. How many carts does Steve have if he can hold 91 redstone blocks total?

4. Zombie villagers have been stomping through your garden, crushing your flowers. If you had 400 flowers in your garden last week and the zombie villagers have crushed $\frac{1}{4}$ of them, how many do you now have?

5. Every year a villager near you adds 2 feet to the height of her house. If her house is currently 10 feet high, how high will it be in 7 years?

6. You have stumbled upon a wall of purpur blocks, and soon discover that every third block has a hostile shulker hidden inside it. If there are 1,260 purpur blocks total in the wall, how many shulkers are there?

7. You and 4 other players are trying to cross a river in the jungle biome. You figure out that 12 lily pads can hold the weight of 2 players. How many lily pads will it take for all 5 of you to cross the river?

GIANT'S GUIDE TO PLACE VALUE

Answer the multiplication and division questions below. Write the correct digit in the place value box.

1. $3416 \div 4 =$ _____

Tens

2. $2200 \div 10 =$ _____

Hundreds

3. $19,450 \div 5 =$ _____

Thousands

4. $783 \times 9 =$ _____

Ones

5. $400,325 \div 5 =$ _____

Ten Thousands

6. $375 \div 3 =$ _____

Hundreds

7. $791,000 \div 7 =$ _____

Hundred Thousands

SKIP COUNT CHALLENGE

You've stumbled upon a pigman hiding in the bushes! Find the pattern to fill in the blanks to finish the path and get to your protective armor.

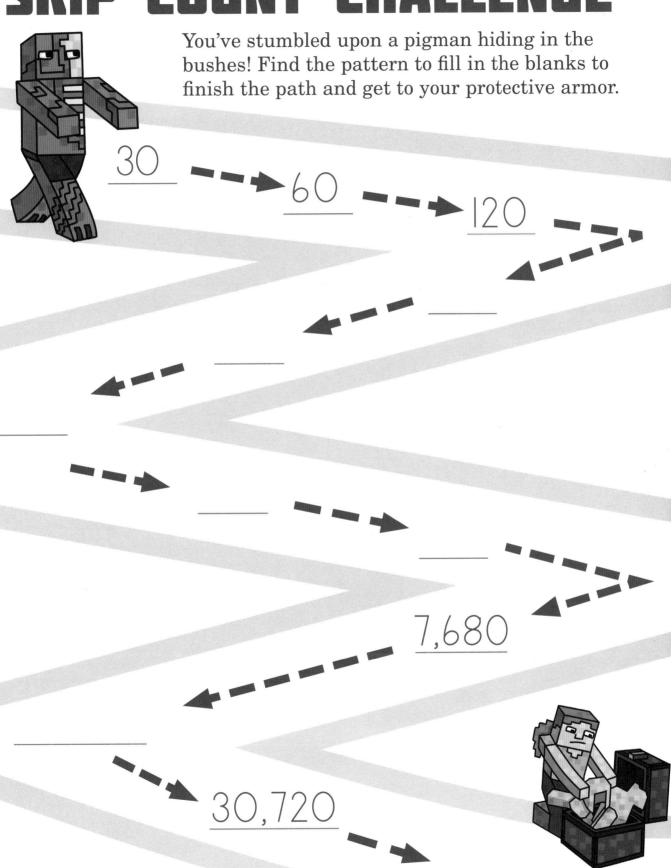

30 ⟶ 60 ⟶ 120 ⟶

_____ ⟵ _____ ⟵

_____

_____ ⟶ _____ ⟶ _____ ⟶

7,680 ⟵

_____ ⟶ 30,720 ⟶ _____

COMPARING FRACTIONS

Can a wolf take down a zombie? Compare the fractions and circle the one that is greater to determine who wins in each battle.

HINT: Draw two same-sized boxes and shade them in to help you compare.

1. $\frac{2}{3}$ $\frac{1}{6}$

2. $\frac{3}{4}$ $\frac{7}{8}$

3. $\frac{1}{4}$ $\frac{1}{3}$

4. $\frac{6}{20}$ $\frac{1}{5}$

5. $\frac{6}{12}$ $\frac{4}{6}$

6. $\frac{1}{3}$ $\frac{4}{8}$

7. $\frac{3}{4}$ $\frac{1}{2}$

8. $\frac{1}{3}$ $\frac{5}{6}$

Who won the most battles overall?

_____

EQUAL FRACTIONS

One week in Steve's world is 140 minutes in real life! Use multiplication and division to fill in the chart and find out how much time Steve spends on each activity.

		Minutes out of a half day (10 minutes)	Minutes out of a day (20 minutes)	Minutes out of a week (140 minutes)
farming		$^1/_{10}$	$^2/_{20}$	$^{14}/_{140}$
fighting		$^3/_{10}$	$—/_{20}$	$—/_{140}$
crafting		$^2/_{10}$	$—/_{20}$	$—/_{140}$
mining		$—/_{10}$	$—/_{20}$	$^{56}/_{140}$

What does Steve spend most of his week doing? _____

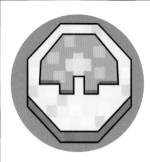

GEOMETRY WORD PROBLEMS

Solve the problems using multiplication and division.

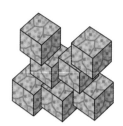

1. If Steve builds a square wall out of lapis lazuli and the wall has an area of 64 square feet, how many feet long is each side of the wall?

2. A Minecrafter's bookcase is shaped like a cube. If each side of that cube is 4 feet long, how many bookcases can you squeeze onto a 144-square-foot floor?

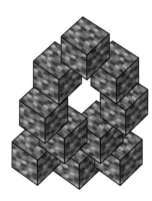

3. Alex has a rectangular fenced-in area that is 4,500 square feet. If the length of the fence is 150 feet, how wide is it?

4. Steve walks the perimeter of his house twice each day to check for zombies and creepers. If all the sides of his house are 24 feet long, how many feet does Steve walk every day?

5. Alex's treasure chest measures 12 feet by 16 feet. She can fit 4 emeralds in every square foot. How many emeralds can she fit in the chest?

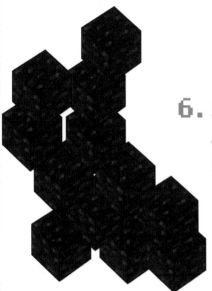

6. Steve built a rectangular obsidian wall that has a perimeter of 20 feet. If the wall is 2 feet long, how wide is it?

7. Steve wants to fit all 18 of his pet cats inside his house. If each cat needs 2 square feet to move freely, how long do the sides of his square house have to be?

ANSWER KEY

Page 4: Multiplication by Grouping

2. 4 x 4 = 16 cows
3. 3 x 7 = 21 chickens
4. 1 x 9 = 9 wolves
5. 6 x 4 = 24 sheep

Page 5: Mystery Message with Multiplication

2. 12
3. 18
4. 24
5. 35
6. 40
7. 16
8. 54
9. 30

Answer: He goes TO DAYSCARE

Page 6: Zombie's Guide to Place Value

2. 4,000 + 600 + 70 + 2
3. 2,000 + 700 + 90 + 8
4. 8,000 + 500 + 40 + 0
5. 3,000 + 100 + 50 + 1
6. 6,000 + 700 + 30 + 6
7. 5,000 + 400 + 50 + 9

Page 7: Math Facts Challenge

7, 14, 21, 28, 35, 42, 49, 56, 63, 70, 77, 84

Page 8: Telling Time

2. 4:40
3. 11:05
4. 9:20
5. 7:10
6. 4:50

Page 9: The Trading Table

1. 32 emeralds
2. 16 emeralds
3. 24 emeralds
4. 48 emeralds
5. The farmer and the butcher.
6. The librarian.
7. The farmer's collection.

Pages 10–11: Geometry Skills Practice

2. 3 x 6 = 18 potions
3. 4 x 4 = 16 experience orbs
4. 2 x 7 = 14 clocks
5. 3 x 7 = 21 creepers
6. 4 x 3 = 12 wolves
7. 1 x 9 = 9 zombies
8. 2 x 6 = 12 spiders
9. 3 x 5 = 15 cows

Hardcore Mode: 7 x 7 = 49 + 5 = 54 experience orbs

Pages 12–13: Multiplication Word Problems

2. 6 buckets
3. 16 planks
4. 18 experience orbs
5. 42 blocks
6. 12 pieces
7. 100 minutes
8. 27 fish
9. 24 bottles

Page 14: Ghast's Guide to Place Value

2. 36, 40
3. 48, 50
4. 15, 20
5. 28, 30
6. 40, 40
7. 63, 60

Page 15: Math Facts Challenge

4, 8, 12, 16, 20, 24, 28, 32, 36, 40, 44, 48

Page 16: Minute Hand Mystery

2. 45 minutes

3. 15 minutes

4. 40 minutes

5. 55 minutes

6. 25 minutes

Page 17: Equal Trade

1. 10 pennies
2. 5 nickels
3. 15 pennies
4. 4 quarters
5. 5 dimes

Page 18: Adventures in Geometry

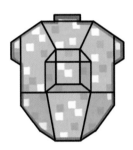

Page 19: Shelter Geometry

1. Area of Alex's wall

8 x 4 = 32

2. Area of Steve's wall

5 x 6 = 30

3. Alex's wall
4. 2 more blocks
5. 62

Page 20: Multiplication by Grouping

1. 3 x 3 = 9
2. 5 x 3 = 15
3. 6 x 3 = 18
4. 2 x 3 = 6
5. 4 x 3 = 12

Page 21: Mystery Message with Multiplication and Division

2. 102
3. 308
4. 62
5. 825
6. 231
7. 603
Answer: Herobrine

Page 22: Enderman's Guide to Place Value

2. E
3. F
4. A
5. C
6. G
7. D

Page 23: Skip Count Challenge

9, 18, 27, 36, 45, 54, 63, 72, 81, 90, 99, 108

Page 24: Telling Time

2. 7:55
3. 4:15
4. 9:20
5. 6:40
6. 12:05
7. 8:30
8. 5:10

Page 25: Spawn Egg Challenge

1. 135
2. 20
3. 188
4. 78
5. 40
6. 212
7. black
8. green and pink
9. 673

Pages 26–27: Equal Parts Challenge

1.

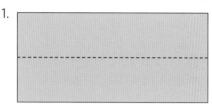

Fraction: ¹/₂

2.

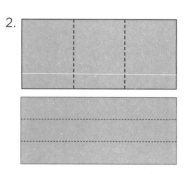

Fraction: ¹/₃

3.

Fraction: ¹/₄

Page 28: Mystery Message with Multiplication

2. 360

3. 243

4. 342

5. 246

6. 368

7. 336

8. 234

9. 350

10. 468

11. 328

Answer: Square Dancing

Page 29: Multiplication and Division Mystery Number

2. 48	3. 10	4. 7	5. 5	6. 4
7. 4	8. 5	9. 3	10. 7	

Page 30: Snow Golem's Number Challenge

1. 43 x 3

2. 642÷2

3. 875÷5

4. 51x8

5. 26x9

Page 31: Skip Count Challenge

6, 12, 18, 24, 30, 36, 42, 48, 54, 60, 66, 72, 78, 84, 90

Pages 32–33: Creating Potions

1. 9, 9

2. 8, 20

3. 42, 54

4. 36, 63

Night Vision Potion	8	12	16	20
Fermented Spider Eyes	14	21	28	35

Pages 34-35: Adventures in Geometry: Perimeter and Area

1. Current perimeter: 26
   New perimeter: 34
2. Current perimeter: 22
   New perimeter: 16
3. Current perimeter: 18
   New perimeter: 26
4. Current area: 36
   New area: 72
5. Current area: 30
   New area: 15
6. Current area: 20
   New area: 40

Pages 36-37: Word Problems

1. 256 carrots
2. 144 seeds
3. 48 pearls
4. 64 baby zombies
5. 29 wheat items
6. 36 minutes
7. 34 trips
8. 126 wheat items

Page 38: Place Value

1. 180 (D)   2. 792 (G)
3. 405 (A)   4. 588 (E)
5. 576 (C)   6. 630 (B)
7. 208 (F)

Page 39: Ghastly Number Challenge

1. 24 x 38
2. 42 x 16
3. 44 x 7
4. 2200 ÷ 10

5. 76 x 10
6. 498 ÷ 2
7. 26 x 20

Pages 40-41: Mob Measurements

2. 30 inches
3. 37 inches
4. 51 inches
5. 18 inches

	Length in meters	Length in cm	Length in mm
	2	200	2,000
	4	400	4,000
	1.5	150	1,500
	2.5	250	2,500
	1	100	1,000

Pages 42-43: Adventures in Geometry

1. clock: obtuse
2. shovel: obtuse
3. ghast: acute
4. chicken: obtuse
5. inventory bar: right
6. potion: right
7. bow and arrow: acute
8. carrot: obtuse
9. pickaxe: acute

Page 44: Multiplication and Division Mystery Number

1. 7   2. 425   3. 137
4. 106   5. 8   6. 378
7. 8   8. 64   9. 78

Page 45: Mystery Message with Multiplication and Division

1. 446
2. 360
3. 89
4. 187
5. 819
6. 920
Answer: boxing

Page 46: Skeleton's Guide to Place Value

1. 131, Hundreds: 1
2. 51, Ones: 1
3. 491, Tens: 9
4. 14, Ones: 4
5. 85, Tens: 8
6. 501, Hundreds: 5
7. 267, Ones: 7

Page 47: Skip Count Challenge

96, 88, 80, 72, 64, 56, 48, 40, 32, 24, 16, 8

Pages 48-49: Animal Tally

1. 14 chickens
2. 56 chickens
3. 17 horses
4. 52 sheep
5. 49 cows
6. 7 cows

7	49
56	14
52	13
17	51

Pages 50-51: Adventures in Geometry

1. bed: parallel
2. railway tracks: parallel
3. door: perpendicular
4. fish: intersecting
5. end crystal: intersecting
6. inventory bar: parallel
7. melon slice: parallel

Pages 52-53: Word Problems

1. 930 pickaxes
2. 210 legs
3. 13 carts
4. 300 flowers
5. 24 feet
6. 420 shulkers
7. 30 lily pads

Page 54: Giant's Guide to Place Value

1. 854, Tens: 5
2. 220, Hundreds: 2
3. 3,890, Thousands: 3
4. 7,047, Ones: 7
5. 80,065, Ten thousands: 8
6. 125, Hundreds: 1
7. 113,000, Hundred thousands: 1

Page 55: Skip Count Challenge

30, 60, 120, 240, 480, 960, 1,920, 3,840, 7,680, 15,360, 30,720, 61,440

Page 56: Comparing Fractions

1. 2/3 is greater, zombie wins
2. 7/8 is greater, wolf wins
3. 1/3 is greater, wolf wins
4. 6/20 is greater, zombie wins
5. 4/6 is greater, wolf wins
6. 4/8 is greater, wolf wins
7. 3/4 is greater, zombie wins
8. 5/6 is greater, wolf wins

Wolf won the most battles overall.

Page 57: Equal Fractions

	Minutes out of a half day (10 minutes)	Minutes out of a day (20 minutes)	Minutes out of a week (140 minutes)
farming	1/10	2/20	14/140
fighting	3/10	6/20	42/140
crafting	2/10	4/20	28/140
mining	4/10	8/20	56/140

Answer: Mining

Pages 58-59: Geometry Word Problems

1. 8 feet long
2. 9 bookcases
3. 30 feet wide
4. 192 feet
5. 768 emeralds
6. 8 feet wide
7. 6 feet long